D1636449

Who Does the Dishes?

Decision Making in Marriage

Winston T. Smith

New Growth Press

www.newgrowthpress.com

New Growth Press, Greensboro, NC 27429
Copyright © 2008 by Christian Counseling & Educational Foundation. All rights reserved. Published 2008

Cover Design: The DesignWorks Group, Nate Salciccioli and Jeff Miller, www.thedesignworksgroup.com

Typesetting: Robin Black, www.blackbirdcreative.biz

ISBN-10: 1-934885-32-0
ISBN-13: 978-1-934885-32-1

Library of Congress Cataloging-in-Publication Data

Smith, Winston T., 1966-
  Who does the dishes? : decision making in marriage / Winston T. Smith.
      p. cm.
  Includes bibliographical references and index.
  ISBN 978-1-934885-32-1
  1. Sex role—Religious aspects—Christianity. 2. Family—Religious aspects—Christianity. 3. Marriage—Religious aspect—Christianity. I. Title.
  BT708.S645 2008
  248.8′44—dc22

                                        2008011756

Printed in Canada
11 12   6 5

Who's responsible for disciplining the kids? Who should be in charge of the checkbook? Who does the laundry?

Is it okay for a wife to work outside the home?

Can the husband stay home and be a homemaker?

How do you decide which family responsibilities belong to you and which belong to your spouse? For many couples, answering these questions is difficult and frustrating. Since marriage is God's idea, it makes sense to look for answers in the Bible. But you won't find there a simple, one-size-fits-all "to-do" list for husbands and wives. Husbands aren't commanded to take out the trash. Wives aren't commanded to change the baby.

That's actually a good thing. Rigidly defined roles would restrict you to tasks that might make sense for your marriage in some circumstances, but not in others. Instead of giving you a list of set duties, God, in the Bible, does something much better. He gives a few basic principles to help you and your spouse define your roles in a godly way no matter what your life is like.

Love Is Your First Responsibility

Love is the bedrock principle. No matter what your culture, traditions, or preferences are, the Bible teaches that in every relationship your first responsibility is love. The apostle Paul, writing to people who were squabbling about their roles in the church, said, "If I speak in the tongues of men and of angels, but have not love, I am only a resounding gong or a clanging cymbal.... and if I have a faith that can move mountains, but have not love, I am nothing" (1 Corinthians 13:1–2).

No matter what your role is, no matter how important you think your job is, no matter how good you are at it, if you're not acting in love, then what you do has no value. *No matter how marital roles are defined, they are only different expressions of love.* Often when we discuss marital roles we never ask the most important questions: Am I expressing love to my spouse through this role? Am I carrying out my role in a way that benefits my spouse? God calls husbands and wives to act in love for the benefit of the other.

Biblical Authority Is About Responsibility and Care

So the overarching principle is love. What else does the Bible have to say about marital roles? When the Bible discusses marital roles, it seems to place a lot of emphasis on authority. Ephesians 5:22–33, Colossians 3:18–19, and 1 Peter 3:1–7 instruct wives to "submit" to their husbands. What role does authority play in marriage?

When you think about the role of authority in marriage, you can go wrong in two ways. You can make the mistake of reducing marriage to a relationship between the ruler and the ruled. That's a distortion of biblical authority. God does not permit husbands to be tyrants or call wives to live as pawns (Ephesians 5:28). Or you can make the opposite mistake and dismiss the place of authority in marriage as so distasteful and destructive that the Bible can't possibly mean what it says about authority in a marriage relationship.

Both of these mistakes can be avoided by understanding how Jesus turned traditional authority roles upside down. The passages in Ephesians, Colossians and 1 Peter aren't just an overview of marriage; they are spelling out guidelines for how authority should work in Christian relationships. In the ancient world, roles were rigidly defined and a sign of one's status and worth. In the radical new kingdom Jesus established, everyone has equal worth and status. Paul wrote in his letter to the Galatians, "You are all sons of God through faith in Christ Jesus....There is neither Jew nor Greek, slave nor free, male nor female, for you are all one in

Christ Jesus" (Galatians 3:26, 28). All children of God have the same spiritual status. Husbands and wives are to view each other with this understanding. Peter instructs husbands to understand their wives as "heirs with you of the gracious gift of life" (1 Peter 3:7).

There is still authority in Jesus' kingdom, but it has a new goal—the care and welfare of others. Once two of Jesus' disciples, James and John, asked Jesus for a favor. They wanted to sit on his right and his left in glory. They wanted to be second-in-command to Jesus! Jesus responded by saying, "You don't know what you are asking." He went on to tell them that he came to suffer and die for the sake of his people, to rescue them from their sin. Finally he said, "You know that those who are regarded as rulers of the Gentiles lord it over them, and their high officials exercise authority over them. Not so with you. Instead, whoever wants to become great among you must be your servant, and whoever wants to be first must be slave of all. For even the Son of Man did not come to be served, but to serve, and to give his life as a ransom for many" (Mark 10:38, 42–45).

Jesus makes a radical distinction between the way he exercises authority and the way the world does. Authority should not be about status and power, as the disciples' request assumes. In Jesus' kingdom, authority is exercised with the attitude of a servant who is working for the welfare of others. God gives authority to governments, officials, mothers, fathers, employers, husbands, etc., so in every area of life someone is ultimately responsible to make sure God's protection and care is being expressed. Those in authority are told to look to Christ as their authority and to imitate him. Christians are to exercise authority in love, for the purpose of serving and helping those under their authority, even at great cost to themselves.

Jesus makes it clear that husbands must not use their authority to serve their own ends of prestige, convenience, comfort, and control. You are God's person on the scene to ensure God's care and protection. Biblical authority is always exercised to care for and nurture those under that authority. When you exercise authority only to care for and nurture yourself, you are doing the exact opposite of what Jesus is calling you to do.

This understanding of biblical authority makes it easier to understand what submission looks like in a marriage relationship. God is asking wives to allow their husbands to love and care for them. This will look different in each marriage, but the bedrock principle will be the same—love. When you are struggling in your relationship with your spouse, return to that principle. Ask yourself, in the context of the role God has given you in your marriage, *How am I expressing love to my spouse?*

Practical Strategies for Change

How do you express love through your role as a husband or a wife? The exact details will differ for each marriage, but there are specific things you and your spouse can do and specific things you should each try to avoid, as you live out your differing roles.

The Role of the Husband

1. *Serve your wife with sacrificial love.* The Bible doesn't give a detailed list of duties, but summarizes all of them under the banner of love. In Ephesians 5, probably the most studied text of the Bible about marriage, the word "love" is used seven times in the space of nine verses to explain the role of the husband. The husband is told to know and imitate Jesus' example of loving the church. Your love is to be sacrificial, placing the needs of your wife above your own (Ephesians 5:25–33).

2. *The goal of your love should be to build up your wife and help her grow as a Christian.* Instead of offering a rigid description of duties, God, in his Word, points you to your most basic responsibility: promoting the welfare of others in love. As long as your goal is love, God gives you the freedom and the latitude to work out the details of your life with your spouse in many different ways (Ephesians 5:25–27).

3. *Don't use your authority to hinder your wife's growth.* Some husbands use their authority in a controlling way and insist on making all the decisions in their marriage. But doing this will not allow your wife to grow in wisdom (or for you to benefit from her wisdom). This also keeps your wife from developing her own relationship with Christ. Part of nurturing others is letting them exercise their own faith by making choices, sometimes even bad ones. God has called you to protect your wife, but don't use that as an excuse for trying to control everything she does. Your wife needs to face situations that require her to trust God, grow in wisdom, and learn responsibility. Sometimes our desire to control others

reveals our own lack of trust in God rather than another's "rebellious attitude."

4. *Get to know your wife.* You can't make wise decisions about how to love your wife if you don't know what her life is like. You must know her hopes, dreams, fears, wants, strengths, and weaknesses. If you haven't listened thoughtfully to the concerns of your wife and worked to understand them, you can't be confident you know what's best for her. And if you aren't listening to your wife and understanding her, she won't be confident your advice is useful. Patient, careful communication allows a couple to build unity in marriage and makes one-sided decision making unnecessary.

Remember, you are merely a steward of God's authority, and you are called to use it only for his goals and purposes. You are forbidden to exercise authority in your own self-interest. As you follow Jesus, expect your authority to be costly. Exercising authority means laying aside your own welfare for the sake of others. Never make decisions out of convenience, vindictiveness, or other selfish motives. Make it your daily practice to ask Jesus to help you examine your motives before you exercise authority.

Living Out Your Servant Leadership

As you read this, you might be thinking, *But you don't know my wife. She criticizes me all the time.* What does servant leadership look like in a marriage where you feel like you are being constantly attacked? It is painful and frustrating to feel criticized all of the time. When you feel like your best efforts are never good enough, it's easy to withdraw or even give up. But let me encourage you to not give up.

Jesus was regularly criticized and rejected for his best efforts, and we know his best efforts were nothing less than perfect love. Isaiah reminds us, "He was assigned a grave with the wicked, and with the rich in his death, though he had done no violence, nor was any deceit in his mouth" (Isaiah 53:9). Remember, you are exercising your role in a fallen world. Even perfect leadership will not always get you a pat on the back or a word of thanks. That's hard, but you are walking in the steps of your Savior. He is your model and your companion in seasons when discouragement sets in. To be criticized for doing your best is the path of servant-leadership in this age.

Remember, too, that Jesus' leadership is *effective*. You, I, and all other Christians are evidence that persevering through criticism and rejection is powerful and effective. Peter, reflecting on Jesus' rejection writes, "For you were like sheep going astray, but now you have returned to the Shepherd and Overseer of your souls" (1 Peter 2:25). Peter is saying that you are a follower of Christ because Jesus refused to give up in the face of rejection. Instead, he trusted God to be at work through the rejection.

Jesus' perseverance in love, even as he was rejected and despised, is the distinguishing mark of grace. What is God's grace but his determination to love us even though we deserve rejection? In the same way, you show Jesus to your wife when you persevere in loving her, even as you feel rejected and criticized. How you respond to her criticism may be your most powerful way of loving your wife and a testimony to Christ's work in your life.

Also consider that Jesus might be speaking to you about your sins through your wife. Is there something right in her criticism? Sure, it may not be delivered in a loving way or even for loving reasons, but is she putting her finger on things you need to face? Is there a theme that runs through them and unites them? Your wife is in a unique position to see things you can't see in yourself. Being criticized is hard for any spouse, but especially for men. In my experience, men place a high value on their wives' confidence in their abilities. Ask God to help you put on humility and be willing to learn from her, even if she's speaking harshly.

After you've examined yourself, make sure you really understand what's going on with your wife. Don't just respond to her defensively; take the time to understand what's driving her criticism. Sometimes criticism sounds like irritation or anger, but it is really thinly veiled fear. Are her criticisms attempts to get you to respond to her fears? Are criticisms about working too much a way of saying, "I'm afraid you care more about your job than me," or "I'm afraid you're interested in someone at the office"?

Sometimes criticism is a form of unresolved bitterness. Perhaps unresolved hurts from the past that are too discouraging to talk about or have been pushed under the rug are being expressed as low-grade irritation. Maybe a financial blunder you made is showing up now as suspicion and criticism every time the bills are due. Her criticism, particularly its ungodly expression, tells you as much about her as it does about you. Servant-leadership means spending more time understanding how to minister to her than defending yourself.

As you spend time talking and listening to each other, you will find plenty of things to repent of. Ask God and your wife for forgiveness. And learn to pray for your wife. Listen to what's on her heart, and pray that God will work in her as he is in you. As you do this, you will be exercising the servant-leadership God has called you to.

The Role of the Wife

The duties of love that apply to your husband also apply to you. You share in the same calling as your husband. You are called to love your husband and encourage him to mature into the image of Christ. Love must be honest, gentle, patient, and self-controlled. Love always encourages, and sometimes even corrects. This means that, more often than not, your roles will appear identical.

1. *Have the right view of submission.* Just as our notions of authority are often distorted by personal and cultural agendas, our understanding of what it means to submit to authority is often distorted as well. For example, some husbands feel that it's improper for their wives to correct

them. They consider it a sign of disrespect and a lack of submission. But the Bible considers correction one of the most basic responsibilities of love. Leviticus 19:17–18 says, "Do not hate your brother in your heart. Rebuke your neighbor frankly, so you will not share in his guilt....Love your neighbor as yourself." When you gently and humbly correct your husband, you are loving him. Your obligation to love your husband is certainly not less than your obligation to a "neighbor." Your duty to correct in love did not go away when you took your marital vows.

2. *Understand respect as a form of love.* Even in moments of disappointment, decide to respond in love. But remember, love speaks, exhorts, corrects, and says no to evil—the Bible is not condemning you to a life of mousy silence. *If you or your children are being verbally, physically, or sexually abused, love your husband by saying no to his sin.* You need help to do this. Please turn to a trusted family member, friend, or pastor to get the support you need. For more information, see the booklet *Living with an Angry Spouse* by Edward T. Welch (New Growth Press).

3. *Act in love even when you are disappointed.*

Instead of turning from your husband in disappointment, can you think of a way you can turn toward him with encouragement, a kind word, even your prayers? Be aware that the shortcomings of your husband can be an opportunity to stroke your own pride or sense of spiritual superiority and indulge in good old-fashioned grumbling. These responses reveal a lack of respect for God more than your husband. Remember, you have a Savior who trusted God in his worst moments. He can help you in those moments when your trust is running low.

Living Out Your Submission

You might be thinking, *But you don't know my husband. He makes decisions without consulting me all the time, and then tells me I have to do what he says because he is "in charge."* What does submission look like in a marriage where the husband demands obedience?

When the solution to a problem seems to boil down to the question of who is "in charge," it means that more important questions aren't being asked. Take the question, "Do I have to do what he says?" and

17

translate it into a set of concerns. Let's take the example of a husband who wants to move his family across the country. What concerns might be behind the question of who makes the decisions? Here are some concerns that a wife would naturally have:

"Relocating will be very upsetting to the kids. They will lose their friends and have to make new ones."

"What if the schools there aren't as good? It could harm their education."

"I don't want to move away from my friends, my church, or my community."

"What if this new job isn't what it promises to be?"

"What if, as we reach for something that seems better, we find out we've let go of something good and end up worse off?!"

These specific concerns can be summarized as "I'm afraid. I'm not sure this decision is best for our family." Asking the question, "Is this the best decision for our family?" is a much more constructive question than, "Do I have to do what he says?" The issue of what is best for your family is a responsibility that you and your husband share as parents, so it should be discussed thoroughly before any decisions are made.

But there are other important questions to consider as well. How will you guard against the temptation to say no to your husband's decisions simply out of fear? A big change (like the example of moving) will reveal your heart because it will expose many of your desires and fears. Think about the specific concerns you have about your husband's decisions. They may very well be legitimate, but you have to be careful that your concerns don't control you. You have to make decisions out of wisdom and love, not fear and self-protection.

Take the case of a decision to move or not. With a little research, you can find out what schools your children would attend. You can find out how safe they are, how good the teachers are, what percentage of children go on to college, etc. But no amount of research can guarantee that your children won't be miserable about leaving their friends, angry with you, or run with the wrong crowd. A decision to move will require you to wrestle with the fear-provoking reality that you cannot completely control your world or guarantee outcomes. A decision to move will require you to have faith—faith that God will work through your new circumstances, whatever they are, easy or difficult, to bless you and your family.

Your husband is also facing temptations as he makes decisions. If he is considering a new job, it might offer status he never thought he could achieve. It might offer a paycheck that promises to be an avenue to the kind of money and security he has always wanted. Or it might be a convenient way out of a job or situation he would rather flee than face. Only he can tell you for sure, but as his wife you may have a hunch what the factors are and the temptations he is facing. You can help your husband take a look at what the temptations are in the different decisions he is thinking through.

Loving your husband means being a trustworthy companion that will invite him to share openly about how he's wrestling with decisions. It's always possible, as he shares his reasons, you will find comfort in the wisdom he has. Don't assume he's being selfish or shortsighted. Be willing to hear the Lord's wisdom in your husband's words.

Loving your husband also means being willing to share with him your perspective on difficult decisions. You can probably see things he can't. As a mother you are likely to be alert to concerns your husband might miss. You have a different relationship with the kids than he does. You might have a different perspective on what makes the household run. How can you bring your concerns to your husband as wisely and constructively as possible? Sharing your honest concerns with your husband isn't a lack of respect or a failure to submit, but your duty in love. It is a sign of your participation and support in the marriage.

Remember, marital roles should never be reduced to issues of "who is in charge." Instead, you are both responsible to love each other in the ways you are gifted and called. Help your husband to think through decisions with you by sharing with him the wisdom and perspective that only his wife and the mother of his children can offer.

Some Advice for Husbands and Wives

1. *Don't recreate your parents' marriage.* God expects you to recognize and respect the gifts and abilities he has given to you and your spouse. It's very common for couples to create their marriages in the image of their parents' marriages. If your father always managed the money, you may

think this is a task that belongs to husbands. Or if your mother always ironed the clothes, you may feel that all wives should do the same. But the Bible tells us God has given his people a variety of gifts—sometimes in ways that surprise us.

2. *Consider how God has uniquely gifted each of you.* Don't read the traditions of your families or culture into the Scripture and make them mandates for your life together. If you're having difficulty sorting out your marital roles, ask a simple question: How has God gifted me? How has he gifted my spouse? If you're terrible with numbers and can't balance the checkbook, while your spouse can do all of that in her sleep, then let her manage the funds. If your spouse has a particular knack for helping the kids see their faults and pointing them to God for help, then let him use that gift in shepherding your children.

3. *Don't consider any gift either inferior or superior.* When the Corinthian church had difficulty in understanding how to exercise their abilities in their various roles, Paul gave them some very important advice. First, accept God's decisions about who has which ability (1 Corinthians 12:4–

13). Second, be aware of the dangers of fear and pride (1 Corinthians 12:14–31). You shouldn't consider your gifts/roles inferior or less important than others, nor should you consider them superior or more important than others. As Paul says, "All these are the work of one and the same Spirit, and he gives them to each one, just as he determines" (1 Corinthians 12:11).

Reflect Christ to Each Other and the Watching World

Finally, understand that your marital roles, however you define them, must reflect the character of Christ. As you work to nail down the details of your roles, it is easy to lose sight of the big picture. The apostle Peter asks us to recognize differences in our roles, but interestingly he begins his instruction to husbands and wives using the phrase, "in the same way." "Wives, in the same way be submissive to your husbands....Husbands, in the same way be considerate as you live with your wives" (1 Peter 3:1, 7). The "in the same way" that Peter is talking about refers to Christ's service that he explains in detail in 1 Peter 2, where he describes Jesus as the head of his people and also as one who submits to authority.

As Jesus led and submitted, he endured great hardship. But he trusted God to work through even the most difficult moments. Rather than lashing out at the sins of others, Jesus powerfully displayed love, mercy, and patience. Whatever your role, whether it is leading, following, or both, you are called to look to Jesus as your example and the only one who can empower you to live out your ultimate calling to live in love and grace.